QUOTABLE WISDOM

•

Steve Jobs

$$\begin{bmatrix} \text{Q U O T A B L E} \\ \text{W I S D O M} \end{bmatrix}$$

•

Steve Jobs

Edited by
CAROL KELLY-GANGI

FALL RIVER PRESS

New York

FALL RIVER PRESS

New York

An Imprint of Sterling Publishing
387 Park Avenue South
New York, NY 10016

Compilation © 2014 by Fall River Press
Originally published in 2012 as *The Wisdom of Steve Jobs.*

ISBN 978-1-4549-1123-4

Distributed in Canada by Sterling Publishing
c/o Canadian Manda Group, 165 Dufferin Street
Toronto, Ontario, Canada M6K 3H6
Distributed in the United Kingdom by GMC Distribution Services
Castle Place, 166 High Street, Lewes, East Sussex, England BN7 1XU
Distributed in Australia by Capricorn Link (Australia) Pty. Ltd.
P.O. Box 704, Windsor, NSW 2756, Australia

For information about custom editions, special sales, and premium and corporate purchases,
please contact Sterling Special Sales at 800-805-5489 or specialsales@sterlingpublishing.com.

Manufactured in the United States of America

2 4 6 8 10 9 7 5 3 1

www.sterlingpublishing.com

Contents

To John and Emily with love

Introduction

When Steve Jobs passed away on October 5, 2011, after a prolonged battle with pancreatic cancer, it was not unexpected. But the immediate and worldwide response to his death was nonetheless overwhelming. Millions of people all over the world stopped to pause and express their grief for someone most of them never even knew. Moving tributes, letters, flowers, and other mementos were left at Apple® stores everywhere, and technology giants stopped to remember Jobs on their own sites. World leaders, business rivals, journalists, celebrities, and millions of regular people paid tribute to Jobs, lauding him with such terms as "genius" and "visionary." Many turned to the technological devices that he had brought to the market to send messages of heartfelt grief for this American icon. In fact, 10,000 tweets per second about Jobs went out the night of October 5—amounting to the biggest online reaction to any event in recent history. Perhaps Jobs himself would have been humbled and slightly bemused by this unprecedented outpouring.

Steven Paul Jobs' story is well-known and, by all accounts, one that only could have happened in America. Born in 1955, he was given up for adoption by his biological parents to Paul and Clara Jobs, decent working-class people who brought him up along with an adopted sister in a loving household in the suburbs of Silicon Valley. Paul Jobs was a tinkerer, who refurbished old cars and could build anything. He famously designated a portion of his workbench for his young son and taught him the fundamentals of using tools, taking things apart, and putting them back together, which ignited in Jobs a lifelong interest for design, craftsmanship, and electronics. After a rocky start in school, the younger Jobs was awakened to the joys of learning by an inspirational fourth-grade teacher, who saw his inordinate potential. His parents, likewise, came to realize that their son possessed a superior intellect and did whatever they could—including moving to a better school district—to support and encourage him. When Jobs was thirteen, a friend introduced him to Steve Wozniak, known as "Woz," an avid electronics geek who impressed him because Woz knew more about electronics than Jobs did. The two became inseparable.

After Steve dropped out of Reed College, worked as a tech at Atari®, and traveled to India in search of enlightenment, he and Woz stumbled upon the idea of forming a computer company. They started dropping in on the Homebrew Computer Club, where they introduced the computer that Woz had constructed in June 1975. Jobs was the one who immediately saw the business potential in their product. Scrambling for components, a design, and financing, the pair founded the Apple Computer Company with a friend, who quickly backed out. In 1977, Apple was incorporated, and the Apple II was launched as the world's first widely used personal computer. By 1980, Apple went public, raising $110 million in an initial public offering (IPO). By 1982, annual sales soared to $1 billion. In 1984, the iconic Macintosh® was launched.

The bottom fell out for Steve Jobs in 1985 when he found himself ousted from the company that he had co-founded; he had clashed with president and CEO John Sculley, who had secured the backing of Apple's board of directors. Dismayed by the betrayal and the ouster, Jobs sold all but one share of his Apple stock and went to work forming NeXT™, a computer company aimed at constructing high-end computers for the academic market. He also purchased an ailing computer graphics company, Pixar, that under his leadership would go on to revolutionize the animated picture industry and ultimately would make him the single largest Walt Disney Company shareholder.

Meanwhile, in Jobs' absence, Apple foundered and was by all accounts close to bankruptcy when Jobs reemerged at Apple: first as special adviser to then CEO Gil Amelio, next as interim CEO, and finally as the permanent CEO after Apple purchased NeXT and used its cutting-edge software as a basis for a new operating system. Under Jobs' leadership, Apple was saved. Jobs and the company went on to transform multiple industries with such revolutionary products as the iMac®, iPod®, iTunes®, iPhone®, and iPad®—amounting to perhaps the greatest comeback in the history of American business.

Steve Jobs: Quotable Wisdom brings together hundreds of quotations from and about this icon, drawn largely from more than twenty-five years' worth of interviews, presentations, and media coverage. The selections are arranged thematically and reflect the subjects of most importance to him. In the selections, Jobs speaks passionately about Apple. He reflects on the vision and goals of the company, as well as how it has evolved and yet stayed true to its roots over the course of its existence. In extracts from early interviews, he prophetically describes the role of personal computers and the impact they will have on our lives. He also expresses his deeply held views about the true meaning of innovation and design. Showing his penchant for showmanship, he also offers his withering assessments of competitors in the computer industry.

In some selections, Jobs shares his insights on hiring, firing, and the workplace—revealing himself as the legendary taskmaster who demands perfection from others, as well as himself. He provides incisive commentary on the pitfalls of wealth, the problems in education, and the value of perseverance. Elsewhere, excerpts offer a more personal glimpse into Jobs, a fiercely private man. He recalls his childhood and the mood of possibility that existed in California at the tail end of the 1960s. He speaks lovingly about his wife and the life-changing event of having children. Finally, a grouping of quotations from world leaders, business and technology giants, journalists, family, and friends offers accolades and insights into Steve Jobs and his enduring legacy.

Steve Jobs: Quotable Wisdom invites readers to consider the man, full of complexity and contradiction, whose vision and leadership gave us the devices, both useful and elegant, that would forever change how the world communicates.

—CAROL KELLY-GANGI

Early Years

My mother taught me to read before I went to school, so I was pretty bored in school, and I turned into a little terror. You should have seen us in third grade. We basically destroyed our teacher. We would let snakes loose in the classroom and explode bombs. Things changed in the fourth grade, though. One of the saints in my life is this woman named Imogene Hill, who was a fourth-grade teacher who taught this advanced class. She got hip to my whole situation in about a month and kindled a passion in me for learning things. I learned more that year than I think I learned in any year in school. They wanted to put me in high school after that year, but my parents very wisely wouldn't let them.

—*Playboy*, February 1985

Look deeper into Jobs' influences and you see not microchips and circuit boards but India, the Beatles, LSD, and Buddhism.

—"How Apple Revolutionized Our World" by Paul Theroux,
Newsweek, September 5, 2011

After reading an article in *Esquire*, Wozniak and Jobs figured out how to build small blue boxes that mimicked the tones used by phone operators—enabling users to place free long-distance calls at will.…He and Woz sold the boxes in the dorms on the Berkeley campus of the University of California, making some nice pocket money before giving it up for fear of getting busted. It was an early test run at entrepreneurship. Jobs later said that without the blue boxes, there would be no Apple.

—"The Steve Jobs Nobody Knew" by Max Crandale,
Rolling Stone, October 27, 2011

My recollection is we stole the show, and a lot of dealers and distributors started lining up and we were off and running.

—On the 1977 West Coast Computer Faire, *Triumph of the Nerds:
The Rise of Accidental Empires*, PBS documentary, 1996

Woz and I very much liked Bob Dylan's poetry, and we spent a lot of time thinking about a lot of that stuff. This was California. You could get LSD fresh made from Stanford. You could sleep on the beach at night with your girlfriend. California has a sense of experimentation and a sense of openness—openness to new possibilities.

—*Playboy*, February 1985

When I was 12 or 13, I wanted to build something and I needed some parts, so I picked up the phone and called Bill Hewlett—he was listed in the Palo Alto phone book. He answered the phone and he was real nice. He chatted with me for, like, 20 minutes. He didn't know me at all, but he ended up giving me some parts, and he got me a job that summer working at Hewlett-Packard on the line, assembling frequency counters. "Assembling" may be too strong. I was putting in screws. It didn't matter; I was in heaven.

—*Playboy*, February 1985

I met Woz when I was 13, at a friend's garage. He was about 18. He was, like, the first person I met who knew more [about] electronics than I did at that point. We became good friends, because we shared an interest in computers and we had a sense of humor. We pulled all kinds of pranks together.

—*Playboy*, **February 1985**

By the fall of 1975, Woz was proudly showing the pieces of a new printed circuit board, and by the end of the year he had built the second of two boards, both designed to drive a color display. Steve Jobs was impressed. . . . He talked to Woz about turning it into a business, and Woz agreed to build printed circuit boards that a hobbyist could buy and then load up with components to create a "computer." Meanwhile, Woz continued working at HP and Jobs continued his night work at Atari.

—*iCon Steve Jobs: The Greatest Second Act in the History of Business*
by Jeffrey S. Young and William L. Simon, 2005

The total cost of the parts that made up an Apple computer was about $250. It consisted of a printed circuit board, the microprocessor, a memory array of 8 kilobytes, and a number of off-the-shelf integrated circuits. Woz thought they should sell the machines for that price, or at best a little more than the cost of the parts. Steve disagreed. He thought they should double the cost of the parts and add a markup for the dealers.

—*Steve Jobs: The Journey is the Reward* by Jeffrey S. Young, 1987

Woz may have had the know-how, but Steve Jobs certainly had the gumption. When Jobs had an objective, nothing stood in the way of his reaching it. One thing that didn't change over the years was his chutzpah, his aggressive personal willingness to wade right in, to go for the top person, the decision maker.

—*iCon Steve Jobs: The Greatest Second Act in the History of Business* by Jeffrey S. Young and William L. Simon, 2005

Steve Jobs had this silver tongue that could talk anyone into anything. And he was working his tail off. He told me about the prices he was getting for parts, and they were more favorable than the prices HP was paying.

—Alan Baum, friend of Steve Wozniak's who agreed to loan $5,000 to the fledgling company, *Steve Jobs: The Journey is the Reward* by Jeffrey S. Young, 1987

I was lucky—I found what I loved to do early in life. Woz and I started Apple in my parents' garage when I was twenty. We worked hard, and in ten years Apple had grown from just the two of us in a garage into a $2 billion company with over 4,000 employees. We had just released our finest creation— the Macintosh—a year earlier, and I had just turned thirty. And then I got fired. How can you get fired from a company you started? Well, as Apple grew we hired someone who I thought was very talented to run the company with me, and for the first year or so things went well. But then our visions of the future began to diverge and eventually we had a falling out. When we did, our Board of Directors sided with him. So at thirty I was out. And very publicly out. What had been the focus of my entire adult life was gone, and it was devastating.

—Commencement address, Stanford University, June 12, 2005

He's also obnoxious and this comes from his high standards. He has extremely high standards and he has no patience with people who don't either share those standards or perform to them.

—**Bob Metcalfe**, *Triumph of the Nerds: The Rise of Accidental Empires*, **PBS documentary, 1996**

When I wasn't sure what the word charisma meant, I met Steve Jobs and then I knew. He wanted you to be great and he wanted you to create something that was great and he was going to make you do that.

—**Apple Computer Chief Scientist Larry Tesler**, *Triumph of the Nerds: The Rise of Accidental Empires*, **PBS documentary, 1996**

I was very lucky to have grown up with this industry. I did everything in the early days—documentation, sales, supply chain, sweeping the floors, buying chips, you name it. I put computers together with my own two hands. And as the industry grew up, I kept on doing it.

—*BusinessWeek*, **October 12, 2004**

Computers

A computer frees people from much of the menial work. Besides that, you are giving them a tool that encourages them to be creative. Remember, computers are tools. Tools help us do our work better. In education, computers are the first thing to come along since books that will sit there and interact with you endlessly without judgment. Socratic education isn't available anymore, and computers have the potential to be a real breakthrough in the educational process when used in conjunction with enlightened teachers. We're in most schools already.

—*Playboy*, **February 1985**

What a computer is to me is the most remarkable tool that we have ever come up with. It's the equivalent of a bicycle for our minds.

—*Memory & Imagination: New Pathways to the Library of Congress*, **television documentary by Julian Krainin, 1990**

A neighbor down the block named Larry Lang was an engineer at Hewlett-Packard. He spent a lot of time with me, teaching me stuff. The first computer I ever saw was at Hewlett-Packard. They used to invite maybe 10 of us down every Tuesday night and give us lectures and let us work with a computer. I was maybe 12 the first time. I remember the night. They showed us one of their new desktop computers and let us play on it. I wanted one badly.

—Playboy, **February 1985**

Basically they were copier heads that just had no clue about a computer or what it could do. And so they just grabbed defeat from the greatest victory in the computer industry. Xerox could have owned the entire computer industry today. Could have been, you know, a company ten times its size. Could have been IBM®—could have been the IBM of the nineties. Could have been the Microsoft® of the nineties.

—On the technology Xerox possessed that Apple brought to fruition,
Triumph of the Nerds: The Rise of Accidental Empires,
PBS documentary, 1996

A computer is the most incredible tool we've ever seen. It can be a writing tool, a communications center, a supercalculator, a planner, a filer, and an artistic instrument all in one, just by being given new instructions, or software, to work from. There are no other tools that have the power and versatility of a computer. We have no idea how far it's going to go.

—*Playboy*, February 1985

It was one of those sort of apocalyptic moments. I remember within 10 minutes of seeing the graphical user interface stuff, just knowing that every computer would work this way someday. It was so obvious once you saw it. It didn't require tremendous intellect. It was so clear.

—On his 1979 visit to the Xerox® Palo Alto Research Center, California, Smithsonian Institution Oral and Video Histories, April 20, 1995

We think the Mac will sell zillions, but we didn't build the Mac for anybody else. We built it for ourselves. We were the group of people who were going to judge whether it was great or not. We weren't going to go out and do market research. We just wanted to build the best thing we could build.

—*Playboy*, February 1985

Apple

The thing that bound us together at Apple was the ability to make things that were going to change the world. That was very important.

—Smithsonian Institution Oral and Video Histories, April 20, 1995

The roots of Apple were to build computers for people, not for corporations. The world doesn't need another Dell® or Compaq®.

—*Time*, October 18, 1999

I've had lots of girlfriends. But the greatest high in my life was the day we introduced the Macintosh.

—*Esquire*, December 1986

What Apple is, is it's an environment where we can attract the best and the brightest people to come together and sort of have a common vision about how we can change the world, and it's very rare that we can actually put something back into the world.

—*PBS NewsHour*, **April 5, 1985**

I received a letter from a six-and-a-half-year-old boy a few months ago which to me completely sums up what we've accomplished in the last few years. And it reads: "Dear Mr. Jobs: I was doing a crossword puzzle and a clue was 'as American as apple blank.' I thought the answer was computer, but my Mom said it was pie."

—*PBS NewsHour*, **April 5, 1985**

We've never worried about numbers. In the marketplace, Apple is trying to focus the spotlight on products, because products really make a difference....Ad campaigns are necessary for competition; IBM's ads are everywhere. But good PR educates people; that's all it is. You can't con people in this business. The products speak for themselves.

—*Playboy*, **February 1985**

There have only been two milestone products in our industry: the Apple II in 1977 and the IBM PC in 1981. Today, one year after Lisa, we are introducing the third industry milestone product: Macintosh. Many of us have been working on Macintosh for over two years now, and it has turned out insanely great. Until now, you've just seen some pictures of Macintosh. Now I'd like to show you Macintosh in person.

—**Macintosh unveiling, January 24, 1984**

That's simply untrue. As soon as we can lower prices, we do. It's true that our computers are less expensive today than they were a few years ago, or even last year. But that's also true of the IBM PC. Our goal is to get computers out to tens of millions of people, and the cheaper we can make them, the easier it's going to be to do that. I'd love it if Macintosh cost $1,000.

—**On claims that Apple hooks enthusiasts with high prices and then lowers them for the remainder of the market, *Playboy*, February 1985**

[The loss of old companies is] inevitably what happens. That's why I think death is the most wonderful invention of life. It purges the system of these old models that are obsolete. I think that's one of Apple's challenges, really. When two young people walk in with the next thing, are we going to embrace it and say this is fantastic? Are we going to be willing to drop our models, or are we going to explain it away? I think we'll do better, because we're completely aware of it and we make it a priority.

—*Playboy*, **February 1985**

John Sculley ruined Apple, and he ruined it by bringing a set of values to the top of Apple which were corrupt and corrupted some of the top people who were there, drove out some of the ones who were not corruptible, and brought in more corrupt ones and paid themselves collectively tens of millions of dollars and cared more about their own glory and wealth than they did about what built Apple in the first place—which was making great computers for people to use.

—Smithsonian Institution Oral and Video Histories, April 20, 1995

I feel like somebody just punched me in the stomach and knocked all my wind out. I'm only 30 years old and I want to have a chance to continue creating things. I know I've got at least one more great computer in me. And Apple is not going to give me a chance to do that.

—On his ouster from Apple after the board sided with John Sculley, whom Jobs had wooed into becoming CEO, *Playboy*, September 1987

I didn't see it then, but it turned out that getting fired from Apple was the best thing that could have ever happened to me. The heaviness of being successful was replaced by the lightness of being a beginner again, less sure about everything. It freed me to enter one of the most creative periods of my life.

—Commencement address, Stanford University, June 12, 2005

You know, I've got a plan that could rescue Apple. I can't say any more than that it's the perfect product and the perfect strategy for Apple. But nobody there will listen to me.

—*Fortune*, September 18, 1995

If I were running Apple, I would milk the Macintosh for all it's worth—and get busy on the next great thing. The PC wars are over. Done. Microsoft won a long time ago.

—*Fortune*, **February 19, 1996**

My position coming back to Apple was that our industry was in a coma. It reminded me of Detroit in the seventies, when American cars were boats on wheels. That's why we have a really good chance to be a serious player again.

—*Fortune*, **January 24, 2000**

You need a very product-oriented culture, even in a technology company. Lots of companies have tons of great engineers and smart people. But ultimately, there needs to be some gravitational force that pulls it all together. Otherwise, you can get great pieces of technology all floating around the universe. But it doesn't add up to much. That's what was missing at Apple for a while. There were bits and pieces of interesting things floating around, but not that gravitational pull.

—**On Apple's problems in the years before his 1997 return,**
BusinessWeek, **October 12, 2004**

O.K., tell me what's wrong with this place. It's the products! So what's wrong with the products? The products SUCK! There's no sex in them anymore!

—Jobs' first meeting at Apple upon his return, July 1997

Apple has some tremendous assets, but I believe without some attention, the company could, could, could—I'm searching for the right word—could, could die.

—On his return as interim CEO of Apple, *Time*, August 18, 1997

Here's to the crazy ones. The misfits. The rebels. The trouble-makers. The round pegs in the square holes. The ones who see things differently. They're not fond of rules....You can quote them, disagree with them, glorify or vilify them. About the only thing you can't do is ignore them. Because they change things. They push the human race forward. And while some may see them as the crazy ones, we see genius. Because the ones who are crazy enough to think that they can change the world, are the ones who do.

—Original "Think Different" Apple advertising campaign narrated by Jobs, 1997

The campaign was a rallying cry, but it was also a keen expression of the artistic, sensuous, romantic, mystical, inquisitive, seductive, austere and theatrical side of Jobs—adjectives not usually associated with the leader of a technology company. It was these attributes that eventually came to be expressed in Apple's products, which Jobs turned into objects of desire.

—Epilogue, *Return to the Little Kingdom: Steve Jobs, the Creation of Apple, and How It Changed the World* by Michael Moritz, 2009

Nobody has tried to swallow us since I've been here. I think they are afraid how we would taste.

—Apple shareholder meeting, April 22, 1998

Apple has a core set of talents, and those talents are: We do, I think, very good hardware design; we do very good industrial design; and we write very good system and application software. And we're really good at packaging that all together into a product....We're the only people left in the computer industry [who] do that.

—*Rolling Stone*, December 2003

This is not a one-man show.... [T]here's a lot of really talented people in this company who listened to the world tell them they were losers for a couple of years, and some of them were on the verge of starting to believe it themselves. But they're not losers. What they didn't have was a good set of coaches, a good plan. A good senior management team. But they have that now.

—*BusinessWeek*, May 12, 1998

Victory in our industry is spelled survival. The way we're going to survive is to innovate our way out of this.

—*Time*, January 14, 2002

The system is that there is no system. That doesn't mean we don't have process. Apple is a very disciplined company, and we have great processes. But that's not what it's about. Process makes you more efficient.

—*BusinessWeek*, October 12, 2004

I've always wanted to own and control the primary technology in everything we do.

—*BusinessWeek*, **October 12, 2004**

We have a lot of customers, and we have a lot of research into our installed base. We also watch industry trends pretty carefully. But in the end, for something this complicated, it's really hard to design products by focus groups. A lot of times, people don't know what they want until you show it to them.

—*BusinessWeek*, **May 12, 1998**

So what we do every Monday is we review the whole business. We look at what we sold the week before. We look at every single product under development, products we're having trouble with, products where the demand is larger than we can make. All the stuff in development, we review. And we do it every single week. I put out an agenda—80% is the same as it was the last week, and we just walk down it every single week.

—*Fortune*, **March 17, 2008**

It's not about pop culture, and it's not about fooling people, and it's not about convincing people that they want something they don't. We figure out what we want. And I think we're pretty good at having the right discipline to think through whether a lot of other people are going to want it, too. That's what we get paid to do.

—*Fortune*, March 7, 2008

I used to be the youngest guy in every meeting I was in, and now I'm usually the oldest. And the older I get, the more I'm convinced that motives make so much difference. HP's primary goal was to make great products. And our primary goal here is to make the world's best PCs—not to be the biggest or the richest. We have a second goal, which is to always make a profit—both to make some money but also so we can keep making those great products. For a time, those goals got flipped at Apple, and that subtle change made all the difference. When I got back, we had to make it a product company again.

—*BusinessWeek*, October 12, 2004

A creative period like this lasts only maybe a decade, but it can be a golden decade if we manage it properly.

—On the release of the iMac, *Fortune*, January 24, 2000

There's a very strong DNA within Apple, and that's about taking state-of-the-art technology and making it easy for people.

—*The Guardian*, September 21, 2005

This is Jobs' definition of Apple's business model, which survives today across multiple products and product categories: Sell well-designed, well-made technology products that aren't the cheapest on the market, but command dependable loyalty from customers because the Apple brand is a mark of quality.

—*Inside Steve's Brain* by Leander Kahney, 2008

Click. Boom. Amazing!

—Keynote address, Worldwide Developers Conference, August 7, 2006

There are some customers which we chose not to serve. We don't know how to make a $500 computer that's not a piece of junk, and our DNA will not let us ship that. But we can continue to deliver greater and greater value to those customers that we choose to serve. And there's a lot of them.

—On Apple's disinterest in entering the netbook market, October 2008

It pained us to see the music companies and the technology companies basically threatening to take each other to court and all this other crazy stuff. So we thought that rather than sit around and throw stones, we'd actually do something about this.

—Fortune, **May 12, 2003**

It will go down in history as a turning point for the music industry. This is landmark stuff. I can't overestimate it!

—On the iTunes Music Store, *Fortune*, **May 12, 2003**

Every once in a while a revolutionary product comes along that changes everything....One is very fortunate if you get to work on just one of these in your career. Apple's been very fortunate it's been able to introduce a few of these into the world.

—**iPhone announcement, January 9, 2007**

Jobs' product introductions are semiannual events, complete with packed houses, breathless blog dispatches, and celebrity appearances—two hours of marketing performance art. Who else could have the nation panting in anticipation of a cellphone?

—*Fortune*, **March 17, 2008**

A lot of companies have chosen to downsize, and maybe that was the right thing for them. We chose a different path. Our belief was that if we kept putting great products in front of customers, they would continue to open their wallets.

—*Success*, **June 2010**

We don't get a chance to do that many things, and every one should be really excellent. Because this is our life. Life is brief, and then you die, you know? So this is what we've chosen to do with our life. We could be sitting in a monastery somewhere in Japan. We could be out sailing. Some of the [executive team] could be playing golf. They could be running other companies. And we've all chosen to do this with our lives. So it'd better be damn good.

—*Fortune*, **March 17, 2008**

What we do at Apple is very simple: We invent stuff. We make the best personal computers in the world, some of the best software, the best portable MP3/music player, and now we make the best online music store in the world. We just make stuff. So I don't know what impresario means. We make stuff, put it out there, and people use it.

—**Technologizer.com, April 28, 2003**

It's in Apple's DNA that technology alone is not enough. That it's technology married with liberal arts, married with the humanities, that yields us the result that makes our hearts sing.

—iPad 2 event, March 2011

I have always said if there ever came a day when I could no longer meet my duties and expectations as Apple's CEO, I would be the first to let you know. Unfortunately, that day has come....I believe Apple's brightest and most innovative days are ahead of it. And I look forward to watching and contributing to its success in a new role. I have made some of the best friends of my life at Apple, and I thank you all for the many years of being able to work alongside you.

—Resignation as CEO, August 2011

NeXT and Pixar

At NeXT, Jobs and his engineers created a sexy black cube-shaped computer that they launched in 1989 at the Davies Symphony Hall in San Francisco....But there NeXT encountered entrenched competitors such as Hewlett-Packard and Sun Microsystems, which could roll out models faster and at a lower price. NeXT suffered also because the ever-stubborn Jobs refused to include a standard floppy drive in the machine. He insisted, instead, on an optical disk drive that developers refused to support because it was too new to the industry. As a result, they never wrote many applications for NeXT, resulting in Jobs being able to sell only about fifty thousand of the machines before pulling out of the hardware market in 1993 to concentrate on the NeXTStep software.

—*Apple: The Inside Story of Intrigue, Egomania, and Business Blunders*
by Jim Carlton, 1997

It'll make your jaw drop.

—On the first NeXT computer, *The New York Times*, November 8, 1989

It is hard to think that a $2 billion company with 4,300-plus people couldn't compete with six people in blue jeans.

—On Apple's lawsuit against him after his resignation to start NeXT, *Newsweek*, September 30, 1985

For Jobs, the Apple deal provides a fresh start for NeXT and a sense of personal vindication. He sees business as a passion, the pursuit of something worthy; his friends talk of his "need to do something big." Suddenly, with an Apple deal, NeXT might indeed do something big. "Joining Apple," Jobs says, "fulfills the spiritual reasons for starting NeXT."

—"Creating Jobs" by Steve Lohr, *The New York Times Magazine*, January 12, 1997

On December 20, 1996, [Apple CEO Gil] Amelio announced that Apple was buying NeXT for $427 million. Jobs returned to Apple as a "special advisor" to Amelio, to help with the transition. It was the first time Jobs had been at the Apple campus in almost eleven years.

—*Inside Steve's Brain* by Leander Kahney, 2008

[Jobs] also picked up a struggling computer graphics company for $10 million from *Star Wars* director George Lucas, who needed cash for a divorce. Renaming it Pixar, Jobs propped up the struggling company for a decade with $60 million of his own money, only to see it eventually produce a string of blockbusters and turn into Hollywood's premier animation studio.

—Introduction, *Inside Steve's Brain* by Leander Kahney, 2008

They're babes in the woods. I think I can help turn Alvy and Ed into businessmen.

—On Pixar co-founders Alvy Ray Smith and Edwin Catmull,
Time, September 1, 1986

We believe it's the biggest advance in animation since Walt Disney started it all with the release of *Snow White* 50 years ago.

—On *Toy Story*, *Fortune*, September 1995

Toy Story took four years to make, during which time Pixar struggled. Jobs never let up on his colleagues. "You need a lot more than vision—you need a stubbornness, tenacity, belief and patience to stay the course," says Edwin Catmull, a 51-year-old computer scientist and a co-founder of Pixar. "In Steve's case, he pushes right to the edge, to try to make the next big step forward. It's built into him."

—"Creating Jobs" by Steve Lohr, *The New York Times Magazine*, January 12, 1997

Pixar's got by far and away the best computer graphics talent in the entire world, and it now has the best animation and artistic talent in the whole world to do these kinds of film. There's really no one else in the world who could do this stuff. It's really phenomenal. We're probably close to ten years ahead of anybody else.

—Smithsonian Institution Oral and Video Histories, April 20, 1995

In 1995, a week after [*Toy Story*'s] release, Pixar went public and Jobs found himself sitting on stock worth $1.1 billion. Suddenly, Jobs looked like a genius again.

—"The Steve Jobs Nobody Knew" by Max Crandale,
Rolling Stone, October 27, 2011

I don't think you'll be able to boot up any computer today in 20 years. [But] *Snow White* has sold 28 million copies, and it's a 60-year-old production. People don't read Herodotus or Homer to their kids anymore, but everybody watches movies. These are our myths today. Disney puts those myths into our culture, and hopefully Pixar will, too.

—*Time*, August 18, 1997

The people who go to see our movies are trusting us with something very important—their time and their imagination. So in order to respect that trust, we have to keep changing; we have to challenge ourselves and try to surprise our audiences with something new every time.

—*To Infinity and Beyond! The Story of Pixar Animation Studios*
by Karen Paik, 2007

Hiring, Firing, and the Workplace

We attract a different type of person—a person who doesn't want to wait five or ten years to have someone take a giant risk on him or her. Someone who really wants to get in a little over his head and make a little dent in the universe....Everyone here has the sense that right now is one of those moments when we are influencing the future.

—*Playboy*, **February 1985**

When I hire somebody really senior, competence is the ante. They have to be really smart. But the real issue for me is, Are they going to fall in love with Apple? Because if they fall in love with Apple, everything else will take care of itself. They'll want to do what's best for Apple, not what's best for them, what's best for Steve, or anybody else.

—*Fortune*, **March 17, 2008**

My job is not to be easy on people. My job is to take these great people we have and to push them and make them even better. How? Just by coming up with more aggressive visions of how it could be.

—*Fortune*, **March 17, 2008**

Many times in an interview I will purposely upset someone: I'll criticize their prior work. I'll do my homework, find out what they worked on, and say, "God, that really turned out to be a bomb. That really turned out to be a bozo product. Why did you work on that?…" I want to see what people are like under pressure. I want to see if they just fold or if they have firm conviction, belief, and pride in what they did.

—*In the Company of Giants: Candid Conversations With Visionaries of the Digital World* **by Rama Dev Jager and Rafael Ortiz, 1997**

Do you want to sell sugared water for the rest of your life, or do you want to come with me and change the world?

—**Enticing then PepsiCo® CEO John Sculley to become Apple's CEO, 1983**

33

Recruiting is hard. It's just finding the needles in the haystack. We do it ourselves and we spend a lot of time at it. I've participated in the hiring of maybe 5,000-plus people in my life. So I take it very seriously. You can't know enough in a one-hour interview. So, in the end, it's ultimately based on your gut. How do I feel about this person? What are they like when they're challenged? Why are they here? I ask everybody that: "Why are you here?" The answers themselves are not what you're looking for. It's the meta-data.

—*Fortune*, March 17, 2008

I hear you're great, but everything you've done so far is crap. Come work for me.

—**Coaxing Xerox engineer Bob Belleville to join Apple,**
Fortune, **March 17, 2008**

In our business, one person can't do anything anymore. You create a team of people around you.

—**Smithsonian Institution Oral and Video Histories, April 20, 1995**

We hire people who want to make the best things in the world. You'd be surprised how hard people work around here. They work nights and weekends, sometimes not seeing their families for a while. Sometimes people work through Christmas to make sure the tooling is just right at some factory in some corner of the world so our product comes out the best it can be. People care so much, and it shows.

—*BusinessWeek*, **October 12, 2004**

We've got 25,000 people at Apple. About 10,000 of them are in the stores. And my job is to work with sort of the top 100 people, that's what I do. That doesn't mean they're all vice presidents. Some of them are just key individual contributors. So when a good idea comes, you know, part of my job is to move it around, just see what different people think, get people talking about it, argue with people about it, get ideas moving among that group of 100 people, get different people together to explore different aspects of it quietly, and, you know—just explore things.

—*Fortune*, **March 7, 2008**

It's painful when you have some people who are not the best people in the world and you have to get rid of them; but I found that my job has sometimes exactly been that, to get rid of some people who didn't measure up, and I've always tried to do it in a humane way. But nonetheless it has to be done and it is never fun.

—Smithsonian Institution Oral and Video Histories, April 20, 1995

To Apple's legions of admirers, the company is like a tech version of Wonka's factory, an enigmatic but enchanted place that produces wonderful items they can't get enough of. That characterization is true, but Apple also is a brutal and unforgiving place, where accountability is strictly enforced, decisions are swift, and communication is articulated clearly from the top.

—"How Apple Works" by Adam Lashinsky, *Fortune*, May 2011

Jobs himself judges the world in binary terms. Products, in his view, are "insanely great" or "shit." One is facing death from cancer or "cured." Subordinates are geniuses or "bozos," indispensable or no longer relevant. People in his orbit regularly flip, at a second's notice, from one category to another, in what early Apple colleagues came to call his "hero-shithead roller coaster."

—"The Trouble with Steve Jobs" by Peter Elkind, *Fortune*, March 5, 2008

Jobs is more like a demanding, hard-to-please father. It's not just fear and intimidation. Underlings work hard to get his attention and his approval. A former Pixar employee told Kramer [Roderick Kramer, social psychologist at Stanford] that he dreaded letting Jobs down, the same way he dreaded disappointing his father. Some people who work for Jobs burn out, but in hindsight they often relish the experience.

—*Inside Steve's Brain* by Leander Kahney, 2008

In the old days at Apple, some people found Jobs' prodding style inspiring and others found it maddening, with Jobs meddling in the tiniest corporate details. His early days at Pixar were much the same. Pamela Kerwin, who joined the company in 1989 and is now a vice president, recalls how Jobs would run a meeting: "After the first three words out of your mouth, he'd interrupt you and say, 'O.K., here's how I see things.' It isn't like that anymore. He listens a lot more, and he's more relaxed, more mature."

—"Creating Jobs" by Steve Lohr, *The New York Times*, January 12, 1997

Jobs is infamous for his temper, but his considerable charm is often downplayed. He uses both the carrot and the stick to get his team to produce great work. He's uncompromising, and the work has to be of the highest standard. He sometimes insists on things that are seemingly impossible, knowing that eventually even the thorniest problem is solvable. But he's also incredibly charismatic, capable of persuading people to do almost anything.

—*Inside Steve's Brain* by Leander Kahney, 2008

Innovation

Making an insanely great product has a lot to do with the process of making the product, how you learn things and adopt new ideas and throw out old ideas.

—*Playboy*, February 1985

Creativity is just connecting things. When you ask creative people how they did something, they feel a little guilty because they didn't really do it, they just saw something. It seemed obvious to them after a while. That's because they were able to connect experiences they've had and synthesize new things. And the reason they were able to do that was that they've had more experiences or they have thought more about their experiences than other people.

—*Wired*, February 1996

You can't just ask customers what they want and then try to give that to them. By the time you get it built, they'll want something new.

—For Entrepreneur of the Decade Award, *Inc.*, April 1989

Innovation has nothing to do with how many R&D dollars you have. When Apple came up with the Mac, IBM was spending at least 100 times more on R&D. It's not about money. It's about the people you have, how you're led, and how much you get it.

—*Fortune*, November 9, 1998

Innovation comes from people meeting up in the hallways or calling each other at 10:30 at night with a new idea, or because they realized something that shoots holes in how we've been thinking about a problem. It's ad hoc meetings of six people called by someone who thinks he has figured out the coolest new thing ever and who wants to know what other people think of his idea.

—*BusinessWeek*, October 12, 2004

There's an old Wayne Gretzky quote that I love. "I skate to where the puck is going to be, not where it has been." And we've always tried to do that at Apple. Since the very, very beginning. And we always will.

—Frequently (and mistakenly) attributed to hockey's Gretzky by Jobs and dozens of other business leaders, this is a bastardized version of a catchphrase created by Gretzky's dad, Walter

This is what customers pay us for—to sweat all these details so it's easy and pleasant for them to use our computers. We're supposed to be really good at this. That doesn't mean we don't listen to customers, but it's hard for them to tell you what they want when they've never seen anything remotely like it. Take desktop video editing. I never got one request from someone who wanted to edit movies on his computer. Yet now that people see it, they say, "Oh my God, that's great!"

—*Fortune*, January 24, 2000

Technology is nothing. What's important is that you have a faith in people, that they're basically good and smart, and if you give them tools, they'll do wonderful things with them.

—*Rolling Stone*, June 16, 1994

People think focus means saying yes to the thing you've got to focus on. But that's not what it means at all. It means saying no to the 100 other good ideas that there are. You have to pick carefully. I'm actually as proud of many of the things we haven't done as the things we have done.

—*Fortune*, **March 7, 2008**

Picasso had a saying: "Good artists copy, great artists steal." We have always been shameless about stealing great ideas… I think part of what made the Macintosh great was that the people working on it were musicians, poets, artists, zoologists and historians who also happened to be the best computer scientists in the world.

—*Triumph of the Nerds: The Rise of Accidental Empires*,
PBS documentary, 1996

The cure for Apple is not cost-cutting. The cure for Apple is to innovate its way out of its current predicament.

—*Apple Confidential 2.0: The Definitive History of the World's Most Colorful Company* **by Owen W. Linzmayer, 2004**

Apple is in a pretty interesting position. Because, as you may know, almost every song and CD is made on a Mac—it's recorded on a Mac, it's mixed on a Mac, the artwork's done on a Mac. Almost every artist I've met has an iPod, and most of the music execs now have iPods. And one of the reasons Apple was able to do what we have done was because we are perceived by the music industry as the most creative technology company.

—*Rolling Stone*, December 3, 2003

We were very lucky—we grew up in a generation where music was an incredibly intimate part of that generation. More intimate than it had been, and maybe more intimate than it is today, because today there's a lot of other alternatives. We didn't have video games to play. We didn't have personal computers. There's so many other things competing for kids' time now. But, nonetheless, music is really being reinvented in this digital age, and that is bringing it back into people's lives. It's a wonderful thing. And in our own small way, that's how we're working to make the world a better place.

—*Rolling Stone*, December 3, 2003

We used to dream about this stuff. Now we get to build it. It's pretty great.

—Keynote address, Worldwide Developers Conference, June 2004

Apple's market share is bigger than BMW's or Mercedes' or Porsche's in the automotive market. What's wrong with being BMW or Mercedes?

—*Macworld*, February 2, 2004

It was a great challenge. Let's make a great phone that we fall in love with. And we've got the technology. We've got the miniaturization from the iPod. We've got the sophisticated operating system from Mac. Nobody had ever thought about putting operating systems as sophisticated as OS X inside a phone, so that was a real question. We had a big debate inside the company whether we could do that or not. And that was one where I had to adjudicate it and just say, "We're going to do it. Let's try." The smartest software guys were saying they can do it, so let's give them a shot. And they did.

—*Fortune*, March 17, 2008

We had the hardware expertise, the industrial design expertise and the software expertise, including iTunes. One of the biggest insights we have was that we decided not to try to manage your music library on the iPod, but to manage it in iTunes. Other companies tried to do everything on the device itself and made it so complicated that it was useless.

—On iPod design, *Newsweek*, October 14, 2006

We did iTunes because we all love music. We made what we thought was the best jukebox in iTunes. Then we all wanted to carry our whole music libraries around with us. The team worked really hard. And the reason that they worked so hard is because we all wanted one. You know? I mean, the first few hundred customers were us.

—*Fortune*, March 7, 2008

But if we put our store in a mall or on a street that they're walking by, and we reduce that risk from a 20-minute drive to 20 footsteps, then they're more likely to go in because there's really no risk. So we decided to put our stores in high-traffic locations. And it works.

—*Fortune*, March 7, 2008

Originally, we weren't exactly sure how to market the Touch. Was it an iPhone without the phone? Was it a pocket computer? What happened was, what customers told us it was, they started to see it as a game machine. We started to market it that way, and it just took off. And now what we really see is it's the lowest-cost way to the App Store, and that's the big draw. So what we were focused on is just reducing the price to $199. We don't need to add new stuff. We need to get the price down where everyone can afford it.

—*The New York Times*, September 9, 2009

Things happen fairly slowly, you know. They do. These waves of technology, you can see them way before they happen, and you just have to choose wisely which ones you're going to surf. If you choose unwisely, then you can waste a lot of energy, but if you choose wisely it actually unfolds fairly slowly. It takes years.

—*Fortune*, March 7, 2008

I think it's brought the world a lot closer together, and will continue to do that. There are downsides to everything; there are unintended consequences to everything. The most corrosive piece of technology that I've ever seen is called television—but then, again, television, at its best, is magnificent.

—*Rolling Stone*, **December 3, 2003**

These technologies can make life easier, can let us touch people we might not otherwise. You may have a child with a birth defect and be able to get in touch with other parents and support groups, get medical information, the latest experimental drugs. These things can profoundly influence life. I'm not downplaying that. But it's a disservice to constantly put things in this radical new light—that it's going to change everything. Things don't have to change the world to be important.

—*Wired*, **February 1996**

There's nothing that makes my day more than getting an e-mail from some random person in the universe who just bought an iPad over in the UK and tells me the story about how it's the coolest product they've ever brought home in their lives. That's what keeps me going. It's what kept me [going] five years ago, it's what kept me going 10 years ago when the doors were almost closed. And it's what will keep me going five years from now whatever happens.

—**All Things Digital D8 conference, Rancho Palos Verdes, California, June 2010**

Design

It's really hard to design products by focus groups. A lot of times, people don't know what they want until you show it to them.

—BusinessWeek, **May 25, 1998**

When you're a carpenter making a beautiful chest of drawers, you're not going to use a piece of plywood on the back, even though it faces the wall and nobody will ever see it. You'll know it's there, so you're going to use a beautiful piece of wood on the back. For you to sleep well at night, the aesthetic, the quality, has to be carried all the way through.

—Playboy, **September 1987**

We build the whole widget.

> —Referring to Apple's design of its hardware and key software,
> *Fortune*, November 12, 2001

People think…that the designers are handed this box and told, "Make it look good!" That's not what we think design is. It's not just what it looks like and feels like. Design is how it works.

> —*The Guts of a New Machine*, November 30, 2003

To design something really well, you have to get it. You have to really get what it's all about. It takes a passionate commitment to really thoroughly understand something, chew it up, not just quickly swallow it. Most people don't take the time to do that.

> —*Wired*, February 1996

[Miele] really thought the process through. They did such a great job designing these washers and dryers. I got more thrill out of them than I have out of any piece of high tech in years.

> —*Wired*, February 1996

Look at the design of a lot of consumer products—they're really complicated surfaces. We tried to make something much more holistic and simple. When you first start off trying to solve a problem, the first solutions you come up with are very complex, and most people stop there. But if you keep going and live with the problem and peel more layers of the onion off, you can oftentimes arrive at some very elegant and simple solutions. Most people just don't put in the time or energy to get there. We believe that customers are smart and want objects which are well thought through.

—On the design of the iPod, MSNBC/*Newsweek*, October 14, 2006

In most people's vocabularies, design means veneer. It's interior decorating. It's the fabric of the curtains and the sofa. But to me, nothing could be further from the meaning of design. Design is the fundamental soul of a man-made creation that ends up expressing itself in successive outer layers of the product or service.

—*Fortune*, January 24, 2000

We made the buttons on the screen look so good, you'll want to lick them.

—On Mac OS X's user interface, *Fortune*, January 24, 2000

A lot of people in our industry haven't had very diverse experiences. So they don't have enough dots to connect, and they end up with very linear solutions without a broad perspective on the problem. The broader one's understanding of the human experience, the better design we will have.

—*Wired*, February 1996

Competitors

If, for some reason, we make some giant mistakes and IBM wins, my personal feeling is that we are going to enter sort of a computer Dark Ages for about 20 years. Once IBM gains control of a market sector, they almost always stop innovation. They prevent innovation from happening.

—On the competition between Apple and IBM-compatible computers,
***Playboy*, February 1985**

I wish [Bill Gates] the best, I really do. I just think he and Microsoft are a bit narrow. He'd be a broader guy if he had dropped acid once or gone off to an ashram when he was younger.

—*The New York Times Magazine*, January 12, 1997

Some people are saying that we ought to put an IBM PC on every desk in America to improve productivity. It won't work. The special incantations you have to learn this time are the "slash q-zs" and things like that. The manual for WordStar, the most popular word-processing program, is 400 pages thick. To write a novel, you have to read a novel—one that reads like a mystery to most people. They're not going to learn slash q-z any more than they're going to learn Morse code. That is what Macintosh is all about.

—*Playboy*, **February 1985**

PLAYBOY: Are you saying that the people who made PC don't have that kind of pride in the product?

JOBS: If they did, they wouldn't have made the PC.

—*Playboy*, **1987**

PLAYBOY: What about Epson and some of the Japanese computer makers?

JOBS: I've said it before: The Japanese have hit the shores like dead fish. They're just like dead fish washing up on the shores. The Epson® has been a failure in this marketplace.

—*Playboy*, **February 1985**

Unfortunately, people are not rebelling against Microsoft. They don't know any better.

—*Rolling Stone*, 1994

The only problem with Microsoft is they just have no taste. They have absolutely no taste. And what that means is, I don't mean that in a small way; I mean that in a big way. In the sense that they don't think of original ideas and they don't bring much culture into their product, and you say why is that important? Well, you know proportionally spaced fonts come from typesetting and beautiful books. That's where one gets the idea. If it weren't for the Mac, they would never have that in their products, and so I guess I am saddened, not by Microsoft's success—I have no problem with their success; they've earned their success for the most part. I have a problem with the fact that they just make really third-rate products.

—*The Triumph of the Nerds: The Rise of Accidental Empires*, PBS documentary, 1996. (Jobs called Bill Gates after the documentary aired to apologize—not for saying the comments, but for saying them publicly.)

I had dinner in Seattle at Bill Gates' house a couple of weeks ago. We were both remarking how at one time we were the youngest guys in this business, and now we're the gray-beards.

—*Fortune*, January 24, 2000

They are shamelessly copying us.

—On Microsoft's newest version of Windows®, Apple annual meeting, 2005

We've kept our marriage secret for over a decade.

—On the greatest misunderstanding about Jobs' relationship with Bill Gates, All Things Digital D5 conference, May 30, 2007

Bill built the first software company in the industry, and I think he built the first software company before anybody really in our industry knew what a software company was except for these guys. And that was huge. That was really huge.

—All Things Digital D5 conference, May 30, 2007

We talk about social networks in the plural, but I don't see anybody other than Facebook out there. Just Facebook. They are dominating this. I admire Mark Zuckerberg...for not selling out, for wanting to make a company. I admire that a lot.

—*Steve Jobs* by Walter Isaacson, 2011

What about 2011? Is it going to be the year of the copycats?

—On the rest of the computer industry's attempt to come up with a tablet modeled after the iPad, March 2, 2011

Family and Friends

I was very lucky. My father, Paul, was a pretty remarkable man. He never graduated from high school....He was a machinist by trade and worked very hard and was kind of a genius with his hands. He had a workbench out in his garage where, when I was about five or six, he sectioned off a little piece of it and said, "Steve, this is your workbench now." And he gave me some of his smaller tools and showed me how to use a hammer and saw and how to build things. It really was very good for me. He spent a lot of time with me.

—**Smithsonian Institution Oral and Video Histories, April 20, 1995**

Yet, biological roots aside, Jobs holds a firm belief that Paul and Clara Jobs were his true parents. A mention of his "adoptive parents" is quickly cut off. "They were my parents," he says emphatically.

—**"Creating Jobs" by Steve Lohr, *The New York Times Magazine*, January 12, 1997**

I think it's quite a natural curiosity for adopted people to want to understand where certain traits come from. But I'm mostly an environmentalist. I think the way you are raised and your values and most of your world view come from the experiences you had as you grew up. But some things aren't accounted for that way. I think it's quite natural to have a curiosity about it. And I did.

—*Playboy*, **February 1985**

After the class [where he met his wife, Laurene], Jobs recalls, "I was in the parking lot, with the key in the car, and I thought to myself, 'If this is my last night on earth, would I rather spend it at a business meeting or with this woman?' I ran across the parking lot, asked her if she'd have dinner with me. She said yes, we walked into town and we've been together ever since."

—**"Creating Jobs" by Steve Lohr,** *The New York Times Magazine*, **January 12, 1997**

When Reed was born, he began gushing and never stopped.

—**Mona Simpson, in her eulogy for her brother,** *The New York Times*, **October 30, 2011**

I remember when he phoned the day he met Laurene. "There's this beautiful woman and she's really smart and she has this dog and I'm going to marry her."

—Mona Simpson, in her eulogy for her brother, *The New York Times*, October 30, 2011

Parenthood changes one's world. It's almost like a switch gets flipped inside you, and you can feel a whole new range of feelings that you never thought you'd have.

—Attributed

His house in Palo Alto is a house on a normal street with a normal sidewalk. No big winding driveway. No big security fences…You could walk into the garden in the back gate, and open the back door to the kitchen, which used to not be locked. It was a normal family home. And he said, "I wanted to live in a normal place where the kids could walk, the kids could go over to other people's houses. And I did not want to live that nutso lavish lifestyle that so many people do when they get rich."

—Walter Isaacson, *60 Minutes*, October 23, 2011

Just to try to be as good a father to them as my father was to me. I think about that every day of my life.

—On what he wants to pass on to his children,
The New York Times Magazine, January 12, 1997

I'd never been so tired in my life. I'd come home at about ten o'clock at night and flop straight into bed, then haul myself out at six the next morning and take a shower and go to work. My wife deserves all the credit for keeping me at it. She supported me and kept the family together with a husband in absentia.

—On his return to Apple, *Fortune*, November 9, 1998

We're family. She's one of my best friends in the world. I call her and talk to her every couple of days.

—On his sister, novelist Mona Simpson, *The New York Times Magazine*, January 12, 1997

When you work with somebody that close and you go through experiences like the ones we went through, there's a bond in life. Whatever hassles you have, there is a bond. And even though he may not be your best friend as time goes on, there's still something that transcends even friendship, in a way. Woz is living his own life now. He hasn't been around Apple for about five years. But what he did will go down in history.

—**On Steve Wozniak, *Playboy*, February 1985**

When I hurt my spine and I was in trouble, this package arrived of books and CDs and music and honey from [Steve Jobs'] garden—tons of stuff arrived at the house. And so, yes, he was a captain of industry, a warrior for his companies. But I found him to be a very thoughtful friend, and a wonderfully detailed and interested parent of his kids, and lover of his wife. There were those two sides to him, the warrior, and then the very, very tender and soft-spoken side. I already miss him.

—**U2 singer Bono, *Rolling Stone*, October 7, 2011**

Steve was the most important friend in my life. He had an incredible mind that couldn't be measured or recognized by normal methods. Like art, [what was so great about Steve's thinking was] it couldn't be put into a formula.

—Steve Wozniak, *People*, October 10, 2011

I have made some of the best friends of my life at Apple, and I thank you all for the many years of being able to work alongside you.

—From Jobs' letter of resignation to Apple's board, August 24, 2011

Education

One of the things I feel is that, right now, if you ask who are the customers of education, the customers of education are the society at large, the employers who hire people, things like that. But ultimately I think the customers are the parents. Not even the students but the parents. The problem that we have in this country is that the customers went away. The customers stopped paying attention to their schools, for the most part. What happened was that mothers started working and they didn't have time to spend at PTA meetings and watching their kids' school. Schools became much more institutionalized, and parents spent less and less and less time involved in their kids' education. What happens when a customer goes away and a monopoly gets control, which is what happened in our country, is that the service level almost always goes down. . . . And that's certainly what the public school system is. They don't have to care.

—**Smithsonian Institution Oral and Video Histories, April 20, 1995**

Equal opportunity to me, more than anything, means a great education. Maybe even more important than a great family life, but I don't know how to do that. Nobody knows how to do that. But it pains me because we do know how to provide a great education. We really do. We could make sure that every young child in this country got a great education. We fall *far* short of that. I know from my own education that if I hadn't encountered two or three individuals that spent extra time with me, I'm sure I would have been in jail. . . . I could see those tendencies in myself to have a certain energy to do something. It could have been directed at doing something interesting that other people thought was a good idea or doing something interesting that maybe other people didn't like so much. When you're young, a little bit of course correction goes a long way. I think it takes pretty talented people to do that. I don't know that enough of them get attracted to go into public education. You can't even support a family on what you get paid.

—**Smithsonian Institution Oral and Video Histories,**
April 20, 1995

It makes me feel old, sometimes, when I speak at a campus and I find that what students are most in awe of is the fact that I'm a millionaire. When I went to school, it was right after the sixties and before this general wave of practical purposefulness had set in. Now students aren't even thinking in idealistic terms, or at least nowhere near as much. They certainly are not letting any of the philosophical issues of the day take up too much of their time as they study their business majors. The idealistic wind of the sixties was still at our backs, though, and most of the people I know who are my age have that engrained in them forever.

—*Playboy*, **February 1985**

The most important thing is a *person*. A person who incites your curiosity and feeds your curiosity; and machines cannot do that in the same way that people can. The elements of discovery are all around you. You don't need a computer. Here—why does that fall? You know why? Nobody in the entire world knows why that falls. We can describe it pretty accurately but no one knows why. I don't need a computer to get a kid interested in that, to spend a week playing with gravity and trying to understand that and come up with reasons why.

—On the role of computers in education, Smithsonian Institution Oral and Video Histories, April 20, 1995

The minute I dropped out I could stop taking the required classes that didn't interest me, and begin dropping in on the ones that looked interesting....I decided to take a calligraphy class to learn how to [create the letters]. I learned about serif and sans-serif typefaces, about varying the space between different letter combinations, about what makes great typography great. It was beautiful. Historical. Artistically subtle in a way that science can't capture. And I found it fascinating. None of this had any hope of any practical application in my life. But 10 years later, when we were designing the first Macintosh computer, it all came back to me. And we designed it all into the Mac. It was the first computer with beautiful typography. If I had never dropped in on that single course in college, the Mac would never have multiple typefaces or proportionally spaced fonts.

—**Commencement address, Stanford University, June 12, 2005**

Money and Wealth

In Steve's important fourth-grade year, Imogene Hill once recalled asking her class, "What in the world don't you understand?" . . . Steve raised his hand and said, "I don't understand why all of a sudden we're so broke."

—*Steve Jobs: The Journey is the Reward* by Jeffrey S. Young, 1987

I was worth about over a million dollars when I was twenty-three and over ten million dollars when I was twenty-four and over a hundred million dollars when I was twenty-five, and it wasn't that important because I never did it for the money.

—*Triumph of the Nerds: The Rise of Accidental Empires,*
PBS documentary, 1996

We had very little money and no foreseeable prospects.
One evening after we had splurged on dinner and a movie,
we walked back to our car to discover a $25 parking ticket.
I just turned inside out with despair, but Steve did not seem
to care. He had a deep well of patience when it came to
discouragements. We drove to the ocean. . .where I began
talking about money worries. He gave me a long, exasperated
look, reached into his pockets and took the few last coins and
dollars we had and threw them into the ocean. All of them.

—**Chrisann Brennan (Jobs' first girlfriend and the mother of
his daughter Lisa),** *Rolling Stone*, **October 27, 2011**

I still don't understand it. It's a large responsibility to have more
than you can spend in your lifetime—and I feel I have to spend
it. If you die, you certainly don't want to leave a large amount
to your children. It will just ruin their lives. . . . The challenges
are to figure out how to live with it and to reinvest it back into
the world, which means either giving it away or using it to
express your concerns or values.

—*Playboy*, **February 1985**

I'm not going to let it ruin my life. Isn't it kind of funny? You know, my main reaction to this money thing is that it's humorous, all the attention to it, because it's hardly the most insightful or valuable thing that's happened to me in the past ten years.

—Playboy, **1987**

I make 50 cents for showing up...and the other 50 cents is based on my performance.

—On his CEO salary of $1 at the annual Apple shareholder meeting in 2007, *AppleInsider,* **May 10, 2007**

Being the richest man in the cemetery doesn't matter to me. Going to bed at night saying we've done something wonderful, that's what matters to me. Sometimes when you innovate, you make mistakes. It is best to admit them quickly, and get on with improving your other innovations.

—On the success of Bill Gates and Microsoft, *The Wall Street Journal,* **May 25, 1993**

Bottom line is, I didn't return to Apple to make a fortune. I've been very lucky in my life and already have one. When I was 25, my net worth was $100 million or so. I decided then that I wasn't going to let it ruin my life. There's no way you could ever spend it all, and I don't view wealth as something that validates my intelligence. I just wanted to see if we could work together to turn this thing around when the company was literally on the verge of bankruptcy. The decision to go without pay has served me well.

—On his return to Apple, *Fortune*, January 24, 2000

I'm the only person I know that's lost a quarter of a billion dollars in one year....It's very character-building.

—*Apple Confidential 2.0: The Definitive History of the World's Most Colorful Company* by Owen W. Linzmayer, 2004

I end up not buying a lot of things, because I find them ridiculous.

—*The Independent*, October 29, 2005

The problem with the Internet startup craze isn't that too many people are starting companies; it's that too many people aren't sticking with it. That's somewhat understandable, because there are many moments that are filled with despair and agony, when you have to fire people and cancel things and deal with very difficult situations. That's when you find out who you are and what your values are. So when these people sell out, even though they get fabulously rich, they're gypping themselves out of one of the potentially most rewarding experiences of their unfolding lives. Without it, they may never know their values or how to keep their newfound wealth in perspective.

—*Fortune*, January 24, 2000

Death and Dying

I remember sitting in his backyard in his garden one day and he started talking about God. He said, "Sometimes I believe in God, sometimes I don't. I think it's fifty-fifty maybe. But ever since I've had cancer, I've been thinking about it more. And I find myself believing a bit more. I kind of—maybe it's 'cause I want to believe in an afterlife. That when you die, it doesn't just all disappear. The wisdom you've accumulated. Somehow it lives on." Then he paused for a second and he said, "Yeah, but sometimes I think it's just like an on-off switch. Click and you're gone." He paused again, and he said, "And that's why I don't like putting on-off switches on Apple devices."

—Walter Isaacson, *60 Minutes*, October 23, 2011

When I was 17, I read a quote that went something like: "If you live each day as if it was your last, someday you'll most certainly be right." It made an impression on me, and since then, for the past 33 years, I have looked in the mirror every morning and asked myself: "If today were the last day of my life, would I want to do what I am about to do today?" And whenever the answer has been no for too many days in a row, I know I need to change something.

. . . Death is the destination we all share, no one has ever escaped it. And that is as it should be because death is very likely the single best invention of life.

. . . Remembering that I'll be dead soon is the most important tool I've ever encountered to help me make the big choices in life. Because almost everything—all external expectations, all pride, all fear of embarrassment or failure—these things just fall away in the face of death, leaving only what is truly important. Remembering that you are going to die is the best way I know to avoid the trap of thinking you have something to lose. You are already naked. There is no reason not to follow your heart.

—Commencement address, Stanford University, June 12, 2005

I'm sorry, it's true. Having children really changes your view on these things. We're born, we live for a brief instant, and we die. It's been happening for a long time. Technology is not changing it much—if at all.

—*Wired*, **February 1996**

That was one of the things that came out most clearly from this whole experience [with cancer]. I realized that I love my life. I really do. I've got the greatest family in the world, and I've got my work. And that's pretty much all I do. I don't socialize much or go to conferences. I love my family, and I love running Apple, and I love Pixar. And I get to do that. I'm very lucky.

—*BusinessWeek*, **October 12, 2004**

Some people say, "Oh, God, if [Jobs] got run over by a bus, Apple would be in trouble." And, you know, I think it wouldn't be a party, but there are really capable people at Apple. My job is to make the whole executive team good enough to be successors, so that's what I try to do.

—*Fortune*, **March 7, 2008**

Steve died peacefully today surrounded by his family. In his public life, Steve was known as a visionary; in his private life, he cherished his family.

—Statement from Jobs' family, October 5, 2011

The Wisdom of Steve Jobs

I know people like symbols, but it's always unsettling when people write stories about me, because they tend to overlook a lot of other people.

—*Time*, **October 10, 1999**

Whenever you do any one thing intensely over a period of time, you have to give up other lives you could be living. You have to have a real single-minded kind of tunnel vision if you want to get anything significant accomplished. Especially if the desire is not to be a businessman, but to be a creative person.

—*Esquire*, **December 1986**

You have to trust in something—your gut, destiny, life, karma, whatever. This approach has never let me down, and it has made all the difference in my life.

—**Commencement address, Stanford University, June 12, 2005**

I'm convinced that about half of what separates the successful entrepreneurs from the non-successful ones is pure perseverance. It is so hard. You put so much of your life into this thing. There are such rough moments in time that I think most people give up. I don't blame them. It's really tough and it consumes your life. If you've got a family and you're in the early days of a company, I can't imagine how one could do it. I'm sure it's been done, but it's rough. It's pretty much an 18-hour day job, seven days a week for awhile. Unless you have a lot of passion about this, you're not going to survive.

—**Smithsonian Institution Oral and Video Histories, April 20, 1995**

It's rare that you see an artist in his 30s or 40s able to really contribute something amazing.

—**(Age 29) *Playboy*, February 1985**

The rewarding thing isn't merely to start a company or to take it public. It's like when you're a parent. Although the birth experience is a miracle, what's truly rewarding is living with your child and helping him grow up.

—*Fortune*, January 24, 2000

That's been one of my mantras—focus and simplicity. Simple can be harder than complex: You have to work hard to get your thinking clean to make it simple. But it's worth it in the end because once you get there, you can move mountains.

—*BusinessWeek*, May 25, 1998

People judge you by your performance, so focus on the outcome. Be a yardstick of quality. Some people aren't used to an environment where excellence is expected.

—*Steve Jobs: The Journey is the Reward* by Jeffrey S. Young, 1987

You can tell a lot about a person by who his or her heroes are.

—*BusinessWeek*, October 12, 2004

I don't think much about my time of life. I just get up in the morning and it's a new day.

—*Fortune*, **November 9, 1988**

It comes from saying no to 1,000 things to make sure we don't get on the wrong track or try to do too much.

—*BusinessWeek*, **October 12, 2004**

You've got to find what you love. And that is as true for your work as it is for your lovers. Your work is going to fill a large part of your life, and the only way to be truly satisfied is to do what you believe is great work. And the only way to do great work is to love what you do. If you haven't found it yet, keep looking. Don't settle. As with all matters of the heart, you'll know when you find it. And, like any great relationship, it just gets better as the years roll on. So keep looking until you find it. Don't settle.

—**Commencement address, Stanford University, June 12, 2005**

I'm an optimist in the sense that I believe humans are noble and honorable, and some of them are really smart. I have a very optimistic view of individuals. As individuals, people are inherently good. I have a somewhat more pessimistic view of people in groups. And I remain extremely concerned when I see what's happening in our country, which is in many ways the luckiest place in the world. We don't seem to be excited about making our country a better place for our kids.

—*Wired*, February 1996

Sometimes life hits you in the head with a brick. Don't lose faith.

—Commencement address, Stanford University, June 12, 2005

It's more fun to be a pirate than to join the navy.

—*Odyssey: Pepsi to Apple* by John Sculley and John A. Byrne, 1987

I think of most things in life as either a Bob Dylan or a Beatles song.

—All Things Digital D5 Conference, May 30, 2007

I would trade all of my technology for an afternoon with Socrates.

—*Newsweek*, October 29, 2001

I think one of the most precious resources we all have these days is free time.

—*ABC News*, June 29, 2005

My self-identity does not revolve around being a businessman, though I recognize that is what I do. I think of myself more as a person who builds neat things. I like building neat things. I like making tools that are useful to people.

—*Esquire*, December 1986

I think if you do something and it turns out pretty good, then you should go do something else wonderful, not dwell on it for too long. Just figure out what's next.

—*NBC Nightly News*, **May 25, 2006**

Your time is limited, so don't waste it living someone else's life. Don't be trapped by dogma—which is living with the results of other people's thinking. Don't let the noise of others' opinions drown out your own inner voice. And most important, have the courage to follow your heart and intuition. They somehow already know what you truly want to become. Everything else is secondary.

—**Commencement address, Stanford University, June 12, 2005**

The Legacy of Steve Jobs

Steve was among the greatest of American innovators—brave enough to think differently, bold enough to believe he could change the world, and talented enough to do it. By building one of the planet's most successful companies from his garage, he exemplified the spirit of American ingenuity. By making computers personal and putting the Internet in our pockets, he made the information revolution not only accessible, but intuitive and fun. And by turning his talents to storytelling, he has brought joy to millions of children and grown-ups alike. Steve was fond of saying that he lived every day like it was his last. Because he did, he transformed our lives, redefined entire industries, and achieved one of the rarest feats in human history: He changed the way each of us sees the world. The world has lost a visionary. There may be no greater tribute to Steve's success than the fact that much of the world learned of his passing on a device he invented, whether a Mac, an iPhone, or an iPad.

—President Barack Obama

It's like the world lost a John Lennon…Steve was clearly the most outstanding business thinker. And almost everybody who's high up in the technology business recognized that, somehow, he had the ability to think out new ways of doing things, not just ways to improve what we have, do a better version of something, but do it in a totally different way that the world would swing towards.

—Steve Wozniak

Apple has lost a visionary and creative genius, and the world has lost an amazing human being. Those of us who have been fortunate enough to know and work with Steve have lost a dear friend and an inspiring mentor. Steve leaves behind a company that only he could have built, and his spirit will forever be the foundation of Apple.

—Apple Chief Executive Tim Cook

Steve, thank you for being a mentor and a friend. Thanks for showing that what you build can change the world. I will miss you.

—Facebook founder Mark Zuckerberg

Steve Jobs was intensely passionate at making an important difference in the lives of his fellow humans while he was on this planet. He never was into money or measured his life through owning stuff. The world knows Steve Jobs as the brilliant genius who transformed technology into magic. A part of Steve still lives within all of us through his beautifully designed products and his no-compromises media experiences. Steve Jobs captured our imagination with his creativity. His legacy is far more than being the greatest CEO ever. A world leader is dead, but the lessons his leadership taught us live on.

—Former Apple Chief Executive John Sculley

I'm truly saddened to learn of Steve Jobs' death. Melinda and I extend our sincere condolences to his family and friends, and to everyone Steve has touched through his work. Steve and I first met nearly 30 years ago, and have been colleagues, competitors and friends over the course of more than half our lives. The world rarely sees someone who has had the profound impact Steve has had, the effects of which will be felt for many generations to come. For those of us lucky enough to get to work with him, it's been an insanely great honor. I will miss Steve immensely.

—Microsoft Chairman Bill Gates

Today is very sad for all of us. Steve defined a generation of style and technology that's unlikely to be matched again. Steve was so charismatically brilliant that he inspired people to do the impossible, and he will be remembered as the greatest computer innovator in history.

—Google® Executive Chairman Eric Schmidt

Steve cared about everything. He had this vigilance. He wanted to delight the user. My team and I had the privilege of designing the first commercial mouse with Steve. I remember that our original prototype used a steel ball, and when you rolled it on the table it could be fairly loud. Steve said that was unacceptable, so we had to coat the ball in rubber, which was a project in itself. But that kind of feedback is a dream for designers—that somebody cares that much....He showed how important it is to pay attention to every aspect of every product. And in doing so, he set the bar for what great design can and should be. Everybody else has had to step up, and they've had to keep on stepping up. Steve demonstrated that design can lead a company to greatness.

—IDEO founder David Kelley, *Wired*, November 29, 2011

From the earliest days of Google, whenever Larry and I sought inspiration for vision and leadership, we needed to look no farther than Cupertino. Steve, your passion for excellence is felt by anyone who has ever touched an Apple product (including the MacBook I am writing this on right now). And I have witnessed it in person the few times we have met.

—Google co-founder Sergey Brin

Steve was a great creative artist. He was also a loving husband and father and I feel privileged to have known him. I enjoyed his quick sense of humor and his love of music. He came to quite a few of our concerts and it was always a pleasure to see him bopping on the sidelines. I once said to him that he must be extremely proud of what he had done. He agreed but said he was even prouder of what he had not done. A great man who will be missed by me and many others.

—Paul McCartney, *Rolling Stone*, October 6, 2011

The intuitive operating systems Jobs created have democratized font design. Right now there's an avalanche of incredibly beautiful typefaces from all over the world that could only be designed on a Mac. Typography, like music, is an art form that embodies a time and place and culture. When type designers plot points on the Mac, they record our moment in time—all in the contour of a letterform.

—*Thirst* founder Rick Valincenti, *Wired*, November 29, 2011

Steve was a very, very tough and tenacious guardian of the Apple brand, but the thing that endeared him to artists was his insistence that things had to be beautiful. He wasn't going to make ugly things that made profits.

—Bono, *Rolling Stone*, October 7, 2011

Steve Jobs was the Michelangelo, the da Vinci, the Einstein of technology—all neatly rolled into one. Apple has lost a genius and an amazing human being, but the world is a better and more interesting place because of him.

—Rolling Stones keyboardist, MotherNatureNetwork.com co-founder Chuck Leavell, MNN.com, October 7, 2011

Steve Jobs is right up there, he is, in many ways, the Bob Dylan of machines, he's the Elvis of the kind of hardware-software dialectic. He's a creature of quite progressive thinking, and his reverence for shape and sound and contour and creativity did not come from the boardroom.

—Bono, *Rolling Stone*, October 7, 2011

Steve was the best of the best. Like Mozart and Picasso, he may never be equaled.

—Investor, technologist, Netscape® co-founder Marc Andreessen, PCMag.com, October 5, 2011

Steve Jobs! Thanks for never settling for the way things were during a life you spent showing us how things could be. O Captain! My Captain!

—Director Kevin Smith, CelebrityTweet.com, October 6, 2011

The world is a better place because of Steve, and the stories our company tells have been made richer by the products he created. He was a dynamic and fearless competitor, collaborator, and friend. In a society that has seen incredible technological innovation during our lifetimes, Steve may be the one true icon whose legacy will be remembered for a thousand years.

—**Time Warner® Chief Executive Officer Jeff Bewkes, Bloomberg.com, October 6, 2011**

Samsung Electronics is saddened to hear of Chairman Steve Jobs' passing and would like to extend our deepest condolences. Chairman Steve Jobs introduced numerous revolutionary changes to the information technology industry and was a great entrepreneur. His innovative spirit and remarkable accomplishments will forever be remembered by people around the world.

—**Samsung Electronics® Chief Executive Choi Gee Sung, Bloomberg.com, October 6, 2011**

Today the world lost a visionary leader, the technology industry lost an iconic legend, and I lost a friend and fellow founder. The legacy of Steve Jobs will be remembered for generations to come.

—**Dell Incorporated Chief Executive Michael Dell,**
Bloomberg.com, October 6, 2011

He was the most amazing product visionary our industry has ever had or probably ever will have.

—**Investor, technologist, Netscape co-founder Marc Andreessen,**
Bloomberg TV, October 7, 2011

I feel honored to have known Steve Jobs. He was the most innovative entrepreneur of our generation. His legacy will live on for the ages.

—**AOL° Founder Steve Case, Twitter, October 5, 2011**

Steve was a teacher to anyone paying attention, and today is a very sad day for everyone who cares about innovation and high standards.

> —**Amazon® Chief Executive Officer Jeff Bezos,** *Los Angeles Times*, **October 6, 2011**

The digital age has lost its leading light, but Steve's innovation and creativity will inspire dreamers and thinkers for generations.

> —**Sony® Chief Executive Officer Howard Stringer,** *Wall Street Journal*, **October 6, 2011**

Jobs has used his natural gifts and talents to remake Apple. He has fused high technology with design, branding, and fashion. Apple is less like a nerdy computer company than a brand-driven multinational like Nike® or Sony: a singular mix of technology, design, and marketing.

> —**Introduction,** *Inside Steve's Brain* **by Leander Kahney, 2008**

Steve Jobs was an iconic entrepreneur and businessman whose impact on technology was felt beyond Silicon Valley. He will be remembered for the innovation he brought to market and the inspiration he brought to the world.

—Hewlett-Packard President and Chief Executive Meg Whitman, Facebook, October 5, 2011

Steve was my hero growing up. He not only gave me a lot of personal advice and encouragement, he showed all of us how innovation can change lives. I will miss him dearly, as will the world.

—Yahoo° co-founder Jerry Yan, *Wall Street Journal*, October 5, 2011

He loved to be the maestro at product presentations. He invented many, many things, but one of the things he invented was this amazing unveiling of products, where the heavens part and the lights shine down and the choir sings hallelujah, and suddenly there's an iPod in his pocket or a Macintosh speaking on stage. And that was part of his showmanship. But the showmanship was able to connect products to us emotionally, just as the design of the product was. So I think it was all part and parcel of his success.

—Walter Isaacson, *PBS NewsHour*, October 28, 2011

Steve Jobs was an extraordinary visionary, our very dear friend, and the guiding light of the Pixar family. He saw the potential of what Pixar could be before the rest of us, and beyond what anyone ever imagined. Steve took a chance on us and believed in our crazy dream of making computer animated films; the one thing he always said was to simply "make it great." He is why Pixar turned out the way we did, and his strength, integrity, and love of life has made us all better people. He will forever be a part of Pixar's DNA. Our hearts go out to his wife, Laurene, and their children during this incredibly difficult time.

—Walt Disney/Pixar Animation Studios® Chief Creative Officer John Lasseter and President Ed Catmull, PixarPlanet.com, October 5, 2011

Steve Jobs was a great friend as well as a trusted advisor. His legacy will extend far beyond the products he created or the businesses he built. It will be the millions of people he inspired, the lives he changed, and the culture he defined. Steve was such an "original," with a thoroughly creative, imaginative mind that defined an era. Despite all he accomplished, it feels like he was just getting started. With his passing the world has lost a rare original, Disney has lost a member of our family, and I have lost a great friend.

—Disney President and CEO Bob Iger, ABCNews.com, October 5, 2011

The magic of Steve was that while others simply accepted the status quo, he saw the true potential in everything he touched and never compromised on that vision.

—Filmmaker George Lucas, ABCNews.com, October 5, 2011

As much as anyone in any walk of life in the early 21st century he changed people's lives simply by imagination and determination. His memory will serve as a symbol of what the human mind can achieve.

—Former British Prime Minister Tony Blair, TonyBlairOffice.org, October 6, 2011

His capacity to revolutionize entire economic fields through the power of his imagination and technology is a source of inspiration for millions of engineers and businesspeople around the world. Inspired and inspiring, Steve Jobs will remain as one of the greatest characters of our time.

—French President Nicolas Sarkozy, Facebook, October 6, 2011

Steve Jobs transformed the way we work and play; a creative genius who will be sorely missed. Our thoughts are with his family.

—British Prime Minister David Cameron, Politics.co.uk, October 6, 2011

Tonight, America lost a genius who will be remembered with Edison and Einstein, and whose ideas will shape the world for generations to come. Again and again over the last four decades, Steve Jobs saw the future and brought it to life long before most people could even see the horizon. And Steve's passionate belief in the power of technology to transform the way we live brought us more than smartphones and iPads: It brought knowledge and power that is reshaping the face of civilization. In New York City's government, everyone from street construction inspectors to NYPD detectives have harnessed Apple's products to do their jobs more efficiently and intuitively. Tonight our city—a city that has always had such respect and admiration for creative genius—joins with people around the planet in remembering a great man and keeping Laurene and the rest of the Jobs family in our thoughts and prayers.

—New York City Mayor Michael Bloomberg, NYC.gov, October 5, 2011

Steve Jobs died Wednesday at the age of 56. Within minutes of the announcement, Twitter and other digital channels were flooded with outpourings of grief for a very private man who leaves a very big mark on the world. It is the footprint, not of a manager or philanthropist, but of an entrepreneur. His legacy is that of an individual who used his drive, vision, curiosity, and keen intelligence to follow new possibilities relentlessly without being deterred by the obstacles on his path.

—**Harvard Business School historian Nancy F. Koehn, CNN.com,
October 6, 2011**

Steve Jobs was a great California innovator who demonstrated what a totally independent and creative mind can accomplish. Few people have made such a powerful and elegant imprint on our lives.

—**California Governor Jerry Brown, CA.gov, October 5, 2011**

Steve Jobs was a giant in the world of technology and established the Bay Area as a global center for innovation. He has inspired and changed the Bay Area and the world forever. Steve Jobs was born in San Francisco and his values were reflected in his generous support for results-driven education reform, 21st century philanthropy, and bridging the digital divide for our diverse communities. Our thoughts and prayers are with his wife, Laurene, his family and friends.

—San Francisco Mayor Edwin Lee, SFmayor.org, October 5, 2011

Steve Jobs was a visionary who changed the way we live, an innovator whose products brought joy to millions, a risk-taker who wasn't afraid to challenge the status quo, and an entrepreneur who led one of the most creative companies of our time. His sage advice was respected by policymakers on both sides of the aisle. His courageous fight against cancer brought strength to many. I hope it is a comfort to those who loved him, especially his family, that so many grieve his loss and are praying for them at this sad time.

—U.S. Congresswoman Nancy Pelosi, Pelosi.House.gov, October 5, 2011

The genius of Steve Jobs, a man I've known for 40 years, not only brought to life the visual magic and brilliant storytelling of Pixar, but brought the world one of the most innovative and successful platforms to make movies and TV....If anyone ever wonders whether one person can make a difference, the answer is Steve Jobs. He will be deeply, deeply missed.

—**Former U.S. Senator, current head of Motion Picture Association Chris Dodd, MovieCityNews.com, October 5, 2011**

Great products, Mr. Jobs said, are triumphs of "taste." And taste, he said, is a byproduct of study, observation and being steeped in the culture of the past and present, of "trying to expose yourself to the best things humans have done and then bring those things into what you are doing." His product-design philosophy was not steered by committee or determined by market research. The Jobs formula, according to colleagues, relied heavily on tenacity, patience, belief and instinct. He became deeply involved in hardware and software design choices, which awaited his personal nod or veto.

—*The New York Times*, **October 21, 2011**

Today, we lost one of the most influential thinkers, creators, and entrepreneurs of all time. Steve Jobs was simply the greatest CEO of his generation. While I am deeply saddened by his passing, I'm reminded of the stunning impact he had in revolutionizing the way people consume media and entertainment.

—News Corporation® Chairman Rupert Murdoch, *Los Angeles Times*, October 5, 2011

When you evaluate how technology affects popular culture, its invention is not as important as its adoption. It matters very little that Apple under Jobs didn't invent the personal computer, the portable music player, the smartphone, or the tablet. It doesn't even matter whether Apple produced the best versions of those devices, or whether its ability to persuade came from pure quality or marketing savvy or both. What matters is that Jobs and Apple pushed all four of those devices forward, and particularly in the case of the three portable devices, it was certainly the company that transformed them from something hobbyists had to something it seemed like everybody had.

—NPR.com, October 6, 2011

While Jobs surely ranks as one of the most important figures in business and technology, he's also one of the most influential cultural figures of our time, the motivating force behind the idea that business and work can be primary sources of creativity, fulfillment, and meaning in our lives; the belief that companies can foment cultural change; the notion that engineers and executives can think like artists; and the realization that good design and aesthetics matter in one of the world's most cutthroat industries.

—*Newsweek: Steve Jobs 1955–2011*, **November 2011**

He proved himself the ultimate willful leader, forging his singular vision through a combination of inspiration, unilateralism, and gut instinct. Jobs didn't just create products that instilled lust in consumers and enriched his company. He upended entire industries. Personal computing. The music business. Publishing. Hollywood. All have been radically transformed because of Steve Jobs.

—*Newsweek*, **September 5, 2011**

Rest in peace, Steve Jobs. You've changed forever the world you leave behind.

—Former *CBS Evening News* anchor Katie Couric, Facebook, October 5, 2011

R.I.P. Steve Jobs. You touched an ugly world of technology and made it beautiful.

—Twitter user Matt Galligan

3 Apples changed the World, 1st one seduced Eve, 2nd fell on Newton and the 3rd was offered to the World half bitten by Steve Jobs.

—Anonymous Twitter user

Rest in Peace, Steve Jobs. Kinda can't believe he's gone. Carrying a little part of him in my pocket every day.

—Actress Martha Plimpton, Facebook, October 5, 2011

There are so few people who are undeniably, brilliantly inspiring. Steve Jobs, a man who changed the way we create, the way we communicate, the way we live, was one of those people. I already miss knowing he is out there.

—TV producer J. J. Abrams, Facebook, October 5, 2011

Steve Jobs was the greatest inventor since Thomas Edison. He put the world at our fingertips.

—Director Steven Spielberg, EntertainmentWeekly.com, October 5, 2011

It's the ultimate sadness. First of all, it's a young person who was revered, sometimes feared, but always revered. He was a very special person, and he didn't get to where he was by having people like him all the time. He got to where he was because he had a vision.

—Former Yahoo Chief Executive Officer Carol Bartz, WSJ.com, October 5, 2011

Steve Jobs, in his career at Apple, reminded us that technological progress is but a human invention, subject to human hopes and human dreams and human choice.

—*Esquire*, **December 2011**

I think Steve Jobs would have had hopes and visions for the future, and he set up Apple Computer really to continue on in his dreams. And I hope that Apple always finds great leaders like him. He made a lot of people happy. How many times can you remember products from a company that just made you happy every time you used them?

—**Steve Wozniak,** *CNN,* **October 5, 2011**

Chronology

February 24, 1955 — Born in San Francisco to Joanne Simpson and Adbulfattah John Jandali. Both are graduate students at the University of Wisconsin and decide to give the child up for adoption. He is adopted by Paul and Clara Jobs, who give him the name Steven Paul Jobs.

1971 — Jobs meets Steve Wozniak. The two share an avid interest in electronics and in using electronics to pull pranks. They go on to construct and sell "blue boxes," a device used to make free long-distance calls.

1972 — Graduates from Homestead High School in Los Altos, California.

1972 — Attends Reed College in Portland, Oregon, but drops out after one semester—though he stays and audits some additional classes.

1974 — Gets job at video game company Atari and begins attending meetings of the Homebrew Computer Club along with Steve Wozniak.

1976 — Apple Computer is formed as a partnership between Jobs, Wozniak, and friend Ronald Wayne, who soon backs out after Wozniak and Jobs construct their first computer circuit board, the Apple I. The pair later sells the computers for $666.66 apiece. Wozniak begins work on Apple II, a fully constructed personal computer.

1977 — Apple is incorporated as Apple Computer Inc., by Wozniak and Jobs and a group of venture capitalists, buying out the original partnership. Apple II is introduced as the world's first personal computer. Sales reach $1 million a year.

1978 — Jobs has daughter Lisa with girlfriend Chrisann Brennan. He disputes paternity until court orders him to take DNA test that proves largely dispositive.

1979 — Jobs and his team visit Xerox PARC and are blown away by a computer with a mouse and the graphical user interface. Development of Macintosh begins.

1980 — Apple goes public. The IPO sells 4.6 million shares and raises $110 million.

1982 — Annual sales soar to $1 billion.

1983 — The Lisa computer is launched as a powerful business tool and the first computer with a mouse, but it meets with poor sales. Jobs woos John Sculley from Pepsi to serve as president and CEO of Apple.

1984 — Apple launches the Macintosh computer to great fanfare. It's the first mass-market GUI computer.

1985 — Jobs is ousted from Apple after falling out with Sculley and having the board turn against him in favor of Sculley.

1985 — Jobs founds NeXT, a company devoted to developing high-end computers for the academic market. Jobs and Wozniak are honored with the National Medal of Technology by U.S. President Ronald Reagan.

1986 — Jobs purchases an ailing computer graphics company from film director George Lucas for $10 million. He renames it Pixar Animation Studios.

1989 — The first NeXT computer goes to market. With a hefty price of $6,500, it sells poorly. Jobs later abandons hardware development to focus solely on software.

1991 — Jobs marries Laurene Powell. They eventually have three children together.

1995 — Pixar releases the movie *Toy Story*, which becomes the highest-grossing film that year. Pixar goes public with an IPO that raises $140 million.

1996 — Apple, in search of new operating system, considers Jobs' software from NeXT along with an operating system from Be, developed by a former Apple executive. Apple ultimately decides to go with Jobs' NeXT software and purchases the company for $430 million.

1997 — Jobs returns to Apple as special advisor to CEO Gil Amelio, who is later pushed out. Jobs is appointed interim CEO and later assumes the position permanently.

1998 — Jobs takes steps to turn things around at Apple, including axing Apple clones, consolidating product lines, and overseeing layoffs. With the launch of the iMac, Apple wages a comeback.

2001 — The first Apple retail stores open. Also, computers using OS X, the updated Mac operating system based on NeXT software, are unveiled. The first iPod goes to market.

2003 — Pixar releases *Finding Nemo*, which goes on to win an Academy Award for Best Animated Feature. Apple launches iTunes Music Store as a way for Mac users to legally buy music online.

2004 — Jobs undergoes surgery for rare form of pancreatic cancer.

2006 — Disney buys Pixar for $7.4 billion, and Jobs becomes Disney's largest shareholder.

2007 — iPhones go on sale, accompanied by huge fanfare.

2009 — Jobs takes medical leave. The public later learns he had a liver transplant.

2010 — Apple introduces, and goes on to sell, 15 million iPads in nine months.

2011 — In August, Jobs resigns as Apple's CEO. He is replaced by Tim Cook and stays on as Chairman.

October 4, 2011 — Cook has his first media event to unveil the iPhone 4GS.

October 5, 2011 — Steve Jobs dies, surrounded by his family.